PAKISTAN

LETTERS FROM AROUND THE WORLD

David Cumming

Photographs by Julio Etchart

CHERRYTREE BOOKS

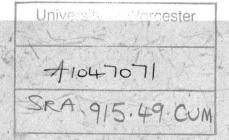

LETTERS FROM AROUND THE WORLD

Titles in this series

AUSTRALIA · BANGLADESH · BRAZIL · CANADA · CHINA · COSTA RICA · FRANCE · INDIA · INDONESIA · ITALY · JAMAICA · JAPAN · KENYA · MEXICO · PAKISTAN · SPAIN

A Cherrytree Book

Conceived and produced by

Nutshell
MEDIA

Intergen House
65-67 Western Road
Hove BN3 2JQ, UK
www.nutshellmedialtd.co.uk

First published in 2004 by
Evans Brothers Ltd
2A Portman Mansions
Chiltern Street
London W1U 6NR

VISIT OUR WEBSITE
www.evansbooks.co.uk
Evans

Editor: Polly Goodman
Designer: Mayer Media Ltd
Map artwork: Encompass Graphics Ltd
All other artwork: Mayer Media Ltd
Series consultant: Jeff Stanfield, Geography
 Inspector for Ofsted
Literacy consultant: Anne Spiring
All photographs were taken by Julio Etchart,
 except: pp8 & 29 (left): Jimmy Holmes.

Acknowledgements
The photographer would like to thank the Shah family, the
staff and pupils of Dheri Naqazchian School, Mian Dheri,
Pakistan, and Waqas Mahmood from the Aga Khan
Foundation, Islamabad, for all their help with this book.

British Library Cataloguing in Publication Data
Cumming, David, 1953
 Pakistan. – (Letters from around the world)
 1. Pakistan – Social life and customs – Juvenile literature
 2. Pakistan – Geography – Juvenile literature
 I. Title
 954.9'105

ISBN 1 8423 4168 5

Cover: Tunweer (third from left) with other players from
 his school cricket team. From the left, they are: Ali,
 Wahid, Rafiq, Rahjid, Ghulam and Mowahid.
Title page: Tunweer carries cut plant food for the goats
 to eat.
This page: Villagers walk along the floodplains of the
 Indus river.
Contents page: Tunweer breaks off a piece of *chapatti*
 to eat.
Glossary page: Tunweer and his brother Zamir walk
 to school.
Further Information page: Tunweer on the batting side of a
 school cricket match.
Index: Tunweer and his friends drinking tea and eating
 chapattis for breakfast.

Printed in China

Contents

My Country

Wednesday, 8 January

c/o Hazara Post Office
Punjab Province
Pakistan

Dear Jo,

Assalam alaikum! (You say 'Ah-sal-um ah-lay-kum'. This means 'hello' in Urdu, an important language in Pakistan.)

My name is Tunweer Shah and I'm 8 years old. I live in the village of Mian Dheri, in northern Pakistan. I have a brother, Zamir, who's 7, and a sister, Sumayya, who's 5.

I'm glad I'm going to be your penpal. I can help you with your class projects on Pakistan.

Write back soon!

From

Tunweer

Here I am (in a white shirt) eating dinner with my mother, brother and sister.

The country that is now Pakistan was only formed in 1947. Before then, it was part of India. In 1971, East Pakistan became a new country, called Bangladesh.

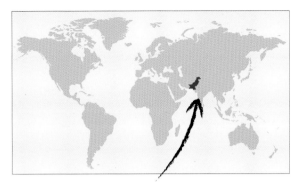

Pakistan's place in the world.

The Karakoram mountains in northern Pakistan are among the highest in the world.

The centre of Pakistan is a wide plain called the Punjab. The Punjab means 'land of five rivers'. It was named after the tributaries of the Indus river, which flow across the plain.

The Punjab is home to most of Pakistan's population. The soil here is good for farming and the rivers provide plenty of water. Most people in the Punjab live in villages like Mian Dheri.

Mian Dheri's houses have flat roofs for storing wood and drying out crops in the sun.

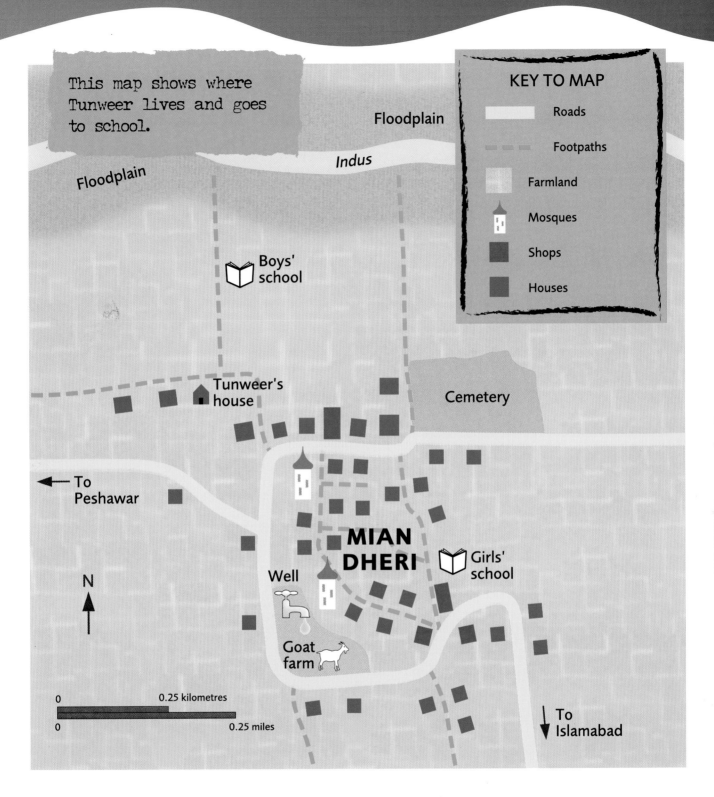

This map shows where Tunweer lives and goes to school.

KEY TO MAP

Roads	
Footpaths	
Farmland	
Mosques	
Shops	
Houses	

Floodplain

Floodplain

Indus

Boys' school

Tunweer's house

Cemetery

To Peshawar

MIAN DHERI

Well

Girls' school

N

Goat farm

0   0.25 kilometres

0   0.25 miles

To Islamabad

Mian Dheri is a large village 0.5 kilometres from the Indus river. There is no bridge near the village, but when the river is low enough, people can walk across to the other side.

Landscape and Weather

Pakistan has many different landscapes and climates. In the northern mountains, winters are freezing while summers are warm. In the Punjab and southern deserts, there are warm winters and very hot summers.

Much of the Karakoram mountain range is covered with snow all year round.

A south-west wind called the monsoon brings rain in July and August. The rain can cause floods.

Most of Pakistan's food is grown on the fertile floodplains beside the Indus river.

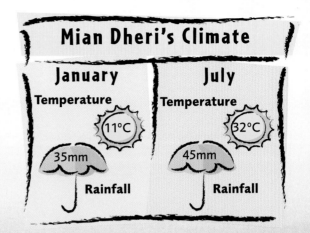

Mian Dheri's Climate

January
Temperature
11°C
35mm
Rainfall

July
Temperature
32°C
45mm
Rainfall

At Home

Tunweer lives in a one-storey house made of bricks. It has a flat roof and two big rooms. One of the rooms is the living room. Tunweer's parents sleep in the other room.

A kitchen, bathroom, toilet and storeroom are in the building next to the house. There is a courtyard in front.

All the houses in Mian Dheri have courtyards like Tunweer's house.

Tunweer, Zamir and Summaya have beds in the sleeping area of the living room.

There are two trees in the courtyard. Tunweer often sits under their shade to do his homework. There is electricity and running water, but Tunweer's family has little furniture and no electrical equipment, except for a radio.

Tunweer's family get all their water from this tap in the courtyard.

11

Tunweer carries some freshly cut plant food for the goats.

Tunweer's dad keeps cows and goats near the house. He uses them for milk and meat. Tunweer's mum makes some of the milk into cheese and yoghurt.

Tunweer and Zamir help to feed the goats. Sumayya helps their mum to keep the house clean and to prepare the meals.

The food is chopped up by a special machine that is powered by electricity. The machine has very sharp blades.

Thursday, 6 February

c/o Hazara Post Office
Punjab Province
Pakistan

Assalam alaikum!

Thanks for your letter. We keep animals, too. There are four goats – two adults and their babies. The baby goats are called kids. They follow me around everywhere.

It's my job to feed the goats. Every morning, I cut and gather up a special crop we grow for them. I take it to Mr Shukat, our neighbour. He's got a machine to chop it up so it's easier for the goats to eat. Do you have any chores?

Write back and tell me.

From

Tunweer

Here I am feeding finely chopped plant food to the goats.

Food and Mealtimes

For breakfast, Tunweer has some bread and jam, with a cup of sweet tea. Lunch is usually lamb or chicken curry, with rice and *chapattis* or nan. The leftovers are heated up for the evening meal, when there is also yoghurt and tea.

Tunweer has breakfast with his brother, sister and three friends.

14

Tunweer shares a lamb curry for lunch with his father, brother, sister and cousins.

Tunweer's mother boils some water on the fire in the kitchen.

In Tunweer's home, food is cooked on a wood-burning fire. Tunweer helps his mother collect the wood from nearby. A few families in the village use bottled gas in their kitchens.

Tunweer and his friends Iqbal and Abbas with fruit drinks from a village shop.

Tunweer's family are Muslims. They do not eat any pork because it is forbidden by their religion, Islam. Muslims consider pigs to be dirty. For this reason, there are no pigs in Pakistan.

Tunweer's mum buys food from the village shops. Tunweer and Zamir bring her vegetables from the family's land. A neighbour has a big oven which Tunweer's mum uses to bake bread.

On this street stall, a woman is frying parathas. These are thick pancakes that are eaten at breakfast.

Wednesday, 5 March

c/o Hazara Post Office
Punjab Province
Pakistan

Hi Jo,

Here's the recipe for *chapattis* that you asked for:

You will need: 250g wheatmeal flour, sieved; 175ml water.

1. Put the flour in a bowl and slowly add the water.
2. Knead the dough until it is smooth. Cover with a damp cloth and leave for 30 minutes.
4. Roll the dough into small balls. Put them on to a floured surface and use a rolling pin to make thin pancakes.
5. Heat a frying pan and add one *chapatti*. Cook on a low heat for 1 minute on either side.
6. Using tongs, lift the *chapatti* and hold it over a low flame or heat for a few seconds, to make it puff up (my mum usually does this bit).

Let me know what you think!

Bye

Tunweer

Here I am with a fresh, warm *chapatti* – lovely on its own or with food.

School Day

It takes Tunweer and Zamir about 10 minutes to walk to school each day.

Tunweer and his brother go to the boys' school just across the fields from their home. Sumayya goes to the girls' school, which is on the other side of the village. In Pakistan, girls and boys go to separate schools because this is what is recommended by Islam.

At 8 a.m. pupils line up for assembly in the school playground.

Tunweer's school doesn't
have enough money for desks
and chairs. The pupils sit
on the floor intead.

Tunweer's school starts at 8 a.m. and finishes at 12.30 p.m. All the boys have to wear the same uniform. It is a dark-grey *salwar khameez* – a long tunic over baggy trousers. It is good for keeping cool during the hot summers.

Tunweer studies two Pakistani languages (Urdu and Punjabi), as well as maths, science and Islam. He plays football in the winter and cricket during the summer months.

The school year starts in September, when the monsoon rains have stopped. The two main holidays are during Ramadan, the Muslim holy month, and August.

Tunweer's dad helps him with his homework, sitting on a traditional Pakistani bed.

Tuesday, 1 April

c/o Hazara Post Office
Punjab Province
Pakistan

Dear Jo,

So football's your favourite sport. Cricket's mine. Everyone here is mad about it. Pakistan comes to a standstill when there's a game on TV. People crowd outside TV shops or go round to neighbours who own a TV. Like you, I play for the school team. We're the champions in this area. I'm one of the best batsmen, with a top score last season of 34. Not out!

Write soon.

From

Tunweer

Here's me scoring a six – well, nearly!

Off to Work

Every day, Tunweer's dad ties up his cows to feed and milk them. The cows are also used to pull a plough in the fields or a cart.

Tunweer's dad is a farmer. Apart from goats, he has a small herd of cows that produce the family's milk. He also has some land outside the village for growing vegetables. He grows enough to feed his family, as well as having some left over to sell to people in the village.

This farmer is preparing the soil for planting seeds.

Other farmers in the village grow rice and wheat. There are also metal workers, carpenters, potters, and several tailors, who have small workshops.

In the cities there are large factories making clothes, and sports and medical equipment. Most of these goods are sold to other countries in Europe and North America.

Kites are so popular in Pakistan that making them is big business. These men are dying the lines that are attached to kites.

Free Time

Only the richer families in Mian Dheri have a television. But for most of the year the weather is too good to stay indoors. Like most children in Pakistan, Tunweer and his friends enjoy playing cricket and flying kites.

Atif is the best batsman among Tunweer's friends.

At the end of a working day, Tunweer's dad usually meets other farmers to drink tea and chat. His mum likes to go to a friend's house. Her friend has a television and a cassette player.

Tunweer's friend Gulzar makes a kite out of paper and thin bits of wood glued together.

Friday, 2 May

c/o Hazara Post Office
Punjab Province
Pakistan

Dear Jo,

What's my favourite hobby? Well, it's cricket again! We don't have a proper pitch in the village, just a patch of land on the side of the road. We've got a proper bat and a ball, but we make the wickets ourselves. They're bits of stick, about the same length, which we put into blocks of mud we've dried in the sun. We don't bother with the horizontal sticks that you put on top.

From

Tunweer

Here I am putting the finishing touches to the wickets with Shahnaz and Umar.

Religion

Like most people in Pakistan, Tunweer and his family are Muslims. From a very young age, Tunweer was taught to pray five times a day.

At home, Tunweer's dad prays on a raised wooden platform. The others pray on mats on the floor. Each time they pray, they face towards Makkah, in Saudi Arabia. Makkah is the holiest city in Islam.

Tunweer's dad prays on a special rug on the platform at home.

In the *madrasah*, children learn Arabic and read the Qur'an.

On Friday, Islam's holy day, Tunweer goes to the mosque with his dad after school. Afterwards he goes to the *madrasah* (the mosque's school), where he learns about the Qur'an. This is the Muslim holy book.

Muslims always leave their shoes outside the mosque to show respect by keeping it clean.

Fact File

Capital city: The capital of Pakistan is Islamabad. It is home to the Shah Faisal mosque, which is the biggest mosque in Pakistan.

Other major cities: Karachi, Lahore, Faisalabad and Rawalpindi.

Size: 803,940km².

Population: 147,663,429.

History: About 4,500 years ago, one of the world's first civilizations began in the Indus Valley, in what is now called Pakistan. Its capital, Mohenjo-Daro, was very advanced for the time. Since then, the region has been ruled by different peoples.

Flag: The star and crescent on Pakistan's flag are traditional symbols of Islam. The white band on the left of the flag represents the other religions followed in Pakistan.

Languages: Urdu is the national language of Pakistan. English and Punjabi are other important languages.

Currency: Pakistani rupee (divided into paisa. 1 rupee = 100 paisa).

Main industries: Cotton, food processing, building materials, paper, shrimps.

Main crop: Wheat is Pakistan's main crop. Cotton, rice, sugar cane, chickpeas, oilseeds, fruits and vegetables are also important.

Highest mountain: K2, or Mount Godwin-Austen (8,611m). This is the world's second-highest mountain.

Longest river: The longest river is the Indus (2,900km).

Main religions: Islam is the largest religion in Pakistan. About 97 per cent of Pakistanis follow it. There are also Christians and Hindus.

Stamps: Pakistani stamps often show famous Pakistanis, the Muslim symbol, or the country's plants.

Glossary

chapatti Thin, round bread that looks like a pancake. It is eaten with a curry.

civilization A group of people with a well-organized way of life.

courtyard A small space surrounded by high walls.

curry Food cooked with spices, like chillies, to make it taste hot.

fertile Soil that is good for farming.

flood Water covering land that is usually dry.

floodplain Land beside a river that is flooded when the river overflows.

Islam A major world faith.

monsoon A strong wind that brings rain.

mosque The building in which Muslims pray.

Muslim A follower of Islam.

nan A type of bread, like a very thick pancake, which is eaten at lunch and dinner.

plain A large area of flat land, often beside a river.

population All the people who live in one place: a country, for example.

Ramadan This is the holy month during which Muslims do not eat or drink anything during the daytime.

salwar khameez The traditional dress of Pakistan.

storey One whole floor of a building.

tributaries Small rivers that flow into a larger one.

wickets Sticks that are bowled at in a game of cricket.

Further Information

Information books:

Country Files: Pakistan by Ian Graham (Watts, 2003)

Country Insights: Pakistan by Eaniqa Khan & Rob Unwin (Hodder Wayland, 2000)

Keystones: Muslim Mosque by Umar Hegedus (A&C Black, 2000)

Rainbows: My Muslim Faith by Khadijah Knight (Evans, 1999)

Sacred Texts: The Qur'an and Islam by Anita Ganeri (Evans, 2003)

Storyteller: Islamic Stories by Anita Ganeri (Evans, 2003)

A World of Festivals: Ramadan & Id-ul-Fitr by Rosalind Kerven (Evans, 1999)

Fiction:

High: Stories of Survival from Everest and K2 edited by Clint Willis (Adrenaline Books, 1999)

Shabanu: Daughter of the Wind (Border Trilogy) by Suzanne Fisher Staples (Econo-Clad Books, 1999)

The Very Hot Samosas: A Story Set in Pakistan by Feroza Mathieson (A&C Black, 1989)

Websites:

CIA Factbook
www.cia.gov/cia/publications/factbook/
Basic facts and figures about Pakistan and other countries.

Index